T0196986

My friend, Johnny Morgan, has done an excellent job of making the case that there are certain postures or positions in one's life where God just moves, and that getting and staying in the correct position to experience God is paramount in the life of a Christian. He does a fantastic job of weaving biblical accounts and personal anecdotes to make his points. There's a depth of thought and insight blended with a practicality to this work and I walked away from reading it both challenged and changed.

Dr. Joseph Vest
Pastor, Freedom Fellowship
Greenville, SC

I enthusiastically encourage every Christian to read this book! If you a brother or sister in Christ, struggling to walk by faith or questioning why you're going through your current difficulties, you need to read this book. It is easy to read and digest. I deeply believe His precious Holy Spirit has guided Brother Johnny to share from the Scriptures and his life experience what we as the body of Christ need to "live out" in our lives individually and corporately. Friend, if you will apply the biblical truths shared within these pages, you will surely "grow in the likeness and knowledge of our Lord Jesus Christ" and impact your world for Him!

Cheryl Jean DeBrot-Erwin
Doctorate of Educational Ministry
Non-Traditional Family Ministry Team Leader
South District Baptist Association, Danville KY
Kentucky Baptist Convention - Mission Service Corp Missionary
Substitute Educator, Three Central Kentucky School Systems

After 15 years of ministry, I wish I would have had access to the book "Get in Position," by Johnny Morgan. Every Christian will have many trials in their life. Johnny's book takes the reader down a path of encouragement through his personal stories and scripture. This easy-reading book encourages its readers to have faith in God's plan for their life. Like the story of Ester, sometimes Christians need to be obedient, put some effort in, then stand back and watch as God orchestrates our lives. If someone is struggling with their faith, this book is a good reminder to "get in position" and wait for God's direction in your life, as God is always working behind the scenes. I would encourage readers to keep a copy of this book on their shelf and come back to it from time to time.

Steve Dismuke
Heritage First Priority Ex Director
Family Pastor

Get In Position

To See God At Work

JOHN N. MORGAN

WESTBOW
P R E S S®
A DIVISION OF THOMAS NELSON
& ZONDERVAN

WestBow Press books may be ordered through booksellers or by contacting:

WestBow Press
A Division of Thomas Nelson & Zondervan
1663 Liberty Drive
Bloomington, IN 47403
www.westbowpress.com
844-714-3454

Scripture quotations are taken from the New King James Version®. Copyright
© 1982 by Thomas Nelson. Used by permission. All rights reserved.

ISBN: 978-1-6642-9048-8 (sc)
ISBN: 978-1-6642-9049-5 (e)

Library of Congress Control Number: 2023901847

Print information available on the last page.

WestBow Press rev. date: 02/28/2023

Contents

Acknowledgements

I'm thankful to my Lord and Savior Jesus Christ, who gave His life so that I could be redeemed. And to the sweet Holy Spirit that helps me daily to be in position to see God at work around me.

I'm thankful to my beautiful wife, who not only is my greatest encourager, but is also willing to step with me by faith into this wonderful journey of following Jesus.

I'm thankful to my many friends who encouraged me in this wild dream of becoming an author.

I'm thankful for my church family, who endured me preaching every chapter of this book to them for weeks.

Foreword

You meet some people, and you automatically click with them. Pastor Johnny Morgan was one of those people for me. His passion for God's Word and his zeal to evangelize the lost is contagious. His partnership in our Central Kentucky GO TELL Crusade helped reach more than 6,000 people with the Gospel that resulted in over 300 making commitments to Christ. Johnny believes that winning souls to Jesus is the dearest thing to God's heart!

As you read "Get in Position," you will understand why Johnny is on a mission to help everyone become followers of Christ. The greatest miracles are not the miracles of glory but the miracles of grace. There is no greater miracle than the miracle of God transforming a sinner into a saint. Johnny has experienced the power and grace that comes only through the shed blood of Jesus Christ on the cross of Calvary. His faith has enabled him to fight through the battles that occur throughout our Christian journey.

I encourage you to read this book. It will help you get in position for God to accomplish His will and purpose for your life.

Rick Gage
GO TELL Ministries

Introduction

Is God the same today as he was in Bible times? Does He still do miracles and do the signs and wonders that we read about in Scripture? Being a pastor, these are the questions ask many times by people who are looking for God. Many feel that He is a far-away God who doesn't come around us, that He is out of reach for us. They do not see Him at work in their lives or around them in society, so they question. One of the biggest challenges for someone working in ministry is to teach people how to look for God in all circumstances. I believe that He is still at work all around us and we will see Him if we **position** ourselves to be in the right places.

Awhile back as I was reading scripture and praying about what God had in store for me to teach at a prayer meeting downtown. I was doing the devotional for the day. I was talking to a friend, who is also a pastor and we were discussing the scriptures that I was planning on using and he recommended a passage for me to look at that he felt went well with my topic. When I read this scripture, the Holy Spirit filled my heart with understanding that this is the reason why so many people are missing out on seeing God at work. God revealed to me that the answer as to how to see God in our lives is to **position** ourselves in the right places to see

Him. This brought to my memory the many times that He showed up in my life.

As a young man I was not raised up in a Christian family. My parents divorced when I was little and both remarried.

Neither my, dad and stepmom, or my mom and stepfather went to church. They didn't teach me about God or His Son Jesus. I was basically, Biblically illiterate. Now I had a few friends that were Christians, but they didn't really talk about it much. I was not put into **position** to know God. They didn't teach me the things that we need to teach our children if we want them to follow Jesus. They did not take me to church or teach me how to pray and talk to God. I didn't know how to lean on Him when I was going through hard times. **I was out of position**. But the good news is that we don't have to stay out of position, no matter what you have going on in your life, God will help you get to where He wants you to be.

God revealed to me that we need to get ourselves into **position** to see Him. He is the same God. He does not change, He can and will do all that He has done before.

God has a plan for every person, and it is up to us to join in. We must put ourselves in the **position** to be where we can receive His blessing and see Him at work. As you go through this book you will see that at times, we will have to put some effort into it. God doesn't want us to just sit back and say "OK God I'm ready. Where are you?" Sometimes God wants us to be patient and wait on Him, even when things around us are hard. He wants us to have faith. And faith is knowing that He will show up at the right time to deliver you.

Chapter 1

Stand Back and Watch

Stand Back and Watch

Have you ever faced a battle so big that you just knew there was no way you could win? Have you ever had the enemy come after you with such a force that it put you in a state of fear? I think that if most of us would think about it, we would have to say that we have been there at some point in our lives. The bigger question would be how did you handle it? Did you give it to God and trust Him for the outcome? Or did you try to face it on your own? God led me to a beautiful passage that I believe will help all of us today as we face the battles in our lives. There is a story about God's people in the Old Testament that tells us of a great King that had a huge battle ahead of him and how he handled it. The story is in **2 Chronicles 20:1-15**, King Jehoshaphat had done some good things as king.

We can read in *1 Kings 22:43* what it says about him that he "did what was right in the sight of the Lord" Some believe that he had put God's kingdom in greater spiritual order than in any time since Solomon. But, isn't that the way it goes, you're working for God doing what you believe He wants you to do, whatever it is, and all of a sudden satan shows up.

Jehoshaphat had news brought to him that a great multitude of people were coming against him. I love the fact that when Jehoshaphat got scared, he sought the Lord. King Jehoshaphat knew that there was no way that he could defeat this enemy, and it scared him. It also says that all Judah came together to seek the Lord. That might be a good idea for the church in America today. And then as all of Judah were seeking the Lord, (the little ones, the wives and the children)

God sent a message to a man of God and gave them an answer right away. King Jehoshaphat did the beautiful prayer; he cried out to God and ask Him if He was still the same God that rules all nations and reminded Him that he had great power and might in His hands. He remembered that God had given the land as an inheritance to the children of Israel. But God didn't give a word for the people to King Jehoshaphat, He sent the word to somebody else. It says that the Spirit of the Lord came upon Jahaziel, one of the kings soldiers, and he spoke these words, "Do not be afraid, for the battle is not yours, but God's."

How many of us are fighting battles today that we shouldn't be fighting? We should have the faith to trust God to deliver us from them. Then in *2 Chronicles 20:16-21* God gave them directions on where to go and then He said something that I'm sure they didn't understand.

"You will not need to fight, just stand still and see the salvation of the Lord." He said go to this place and **position** yourselves and watch Me do what only I can do. Just stand still and watch. Will we do that? Will we believe that God can and will defeat our enemies for us? Will we **position** ourselves where we can watch God do what only He can do?

If only we could have the faith to let God handle it. There are many reasons why we try to fight ourselves. Maybe we think that we can handle it ourselves. Maybe we think that God is too busy taking care of everybody else, so He doesn't have time to handle our problems. We should be more like Jehoshaphat and just cry out to Him.

There was a time in my life that I was wanting to fight a battle for myself. Sherri and I were at a small rural church and God was blessing our ministry there.

The attendance was growing, people were getting baptized. Things were going really good, or so I thought. After finishing VBS one summer, unknown to me, a family had gotten upset about the way things had been done and started talking about us behind our backs. Complaining about the way we were leading. Before I knew anything was wrong, a couple of the men in the church came to my house and informed me that I should resign. There were some very ugly things said about us that were just not true and I wanted so much to defend Sherri and myself. But through much prayer, God told me to leave it to Him and I did. After I resigned I found out later that one of our youth in the church was the one who stood up and defended us.

She stood up in front of the whole church, calling everyone that was involved to come to the alter and ask forgiveness from God and repent.

God will fight for us and sometimes He will use a young, strong, born again, Christian girl to do it. We just have, to have the faith to trust Him and be in **Position** to **Stand Back and Watch**.

Chapter 2

Put Some Effort Into It

Put Some Effort Into It

I believe that there are people everywhere that are wanting to see God do great things in their lives, in the lives of their families, in their churches, in their communities, in this nation. But unfortunately, they don't. Why? I think it could be that we don't have ourselves in **Position** to see Him, so we miss out. Let's talk about a man in the New Testament that did what he had to do to have an encounter with Jesus. In *Luke 19:1-10* it says;

> "Then *Jesus* entered and passed through Jericho.
> ² Now behold, *there was* a man named Zacchaeus who was a chief tax collector, and he was rich. ³ And he sought to see who Jesus was, but could not because of the crowd, for he was of short stature. ⁴ So he ran ahead and climbed up into a sycamore tree to see Him, for He was going to pass that *way.*
>
> ⁵ And when Jesus came to the place, He looked up and saw him, and said to him, "Zacchaeus, make haste and come down, for today I must stay at your house." ⁶ So he made haste and came down, and received Him joyfully. ⁷ But when they saw *it,* they all complained, saying, "He has gone to be a guest with a man who is a sinner."
>
> ⁸ Then Zacchaeus stood and said to the Lord, "Look, Lord, I give half of my goods to the poor; and if I have taken anything from anyone by false accusation, I restore fourfold."

> [9] And Jesus said to him, "Today salvation has come
> to this house, because he also is a son of Abraham;
> [10] for the Son of Man has come to seek and to save
> that which was lost."

We learn that in the city of Jericho there was a small tax collector by the name of Zacchaeus, who was very rich. He got that way by taking tax money from his people (the Jews) and giving it to the Romans. Our scripture tells us that he was a chief tax collector which means he was probably in charge over a whole district.

And many of his own people didn't like him very much, they couldn't understand how anybody could take money from his own people and give it to the Romans. This wealthy man had heard about Jesus and all the things that He was doing and desired to see Him. When he heard that Jesus was coming into town, he went to see Him. But when he got there, the crowd was too big and he was too short to see over everybody, so he climbed up a tree. He did what he had to do to **Position** himself to be where he could see Jesus.

Sometimes when we want to see Jesus, it takes effort. Not only was it embarrassing for a rich man to climb a tree, but it also required him to do something.

What are we willing to do to see Jesus?

You and I both hear people all the time wondering if God really does, do the things He used to in the world.

I believe that if we want to see God at work around us, we need to be like this tax collector and put in the effort. We need to be in **Position** to see Him. Jesus saw this man in the tree and told him *"To hurry and come down, so that He could stay at his house that day,"*

And he did, and the scriptures talk about how Zacchaeus repented and paid back what he had taken. And did you see that in verse 9 what Jesus said?

God used the same word as He used in the passage in 2 Chronicles, *"Today salvation has come to this house,"* The word salvation here could also be translated deliverance. There may be someone that you know and love that needs salvation or deliverance. It just may be you and maybe you are like Zacchaeus and people don't like you very much. Maybe you just need to **Position** yourself to where you can see God show up in your life.

———

I have a friend that is the Missions Pastor at his church and a few years ago he asks me if I wanted to go with a team to Costa Rica. I had never been out of the country at that time and as I prayed about it, I felt that the Holy Spirit was leading me to go, so I said yes.

What I didn't know at that time was that his church didn't want people to just pay for the trip like it was a vacation. Instead they wanted people to get sponsors from their own church or their family and friends. Asking them to not only support you financially, but also to pray for you during the time you were gone. It was a little embarrassing for me to ask others to pay for my mission trip, but I did. Let me tell you that it was one of the greatest blessings for me in my entire life. Going there and seeing God at work in the people there was amazing.

I felt the presence of the Holy Spirit so many times and could see Him at work all around us. I would have never been able to have that experience if I had not been willing to humble myself and **Put Some Effort Into It**.

Chapter 3

Wait for It

Wait for It

In the last chapter we saw how from scripture we know that God wants us to get in **position** to see Him. We talked about how Zacchaeus had to put some effort in it. He had to humble himself and climb a tree. We can see in today's world people are still doing things (getting themselves in position) to help them in life.

I heard an interview with a NASCAR stock car driver, one time. He said that in the long 500-mile races, you could not go out and try to win the race in the very beginning. You had to be patient and wait and **position** yourself at the end of the race to win. He said you want to be close to the front within the last three or four laps. That means you need to take care of your equipment, you must be ready yourself mentally, and sometimes you might have to let someone else lead for a while.

All of these things can also be important in our spiritual lives as well.

The reason I told you this is so that as we read todays scripture you will understand that sometimes you can't be in a hurry to see God at work. Sometimes you just have to put yourself in **position** and wait. You need to be patient. Even if things are not going good for you, or if people aren't treating your right. So, I want us to look at some people in scripture that had to wait for a while before they were able to see God move in their lives.

In *Daniel 1:1-21* we can read about Daniel, Hananiah, Mishael, and Azariah, they are 4 Hebrew boys who were captured and taken to Babylon to be trained to be in service to the king. These guys, scripture say, were good looking, gifted in wisdom, and possessed knowledge.

The king appointed for them the best food and drink from

his own table and 3 years of training to serve him. He also took away their Hebrew names and gave them Babylonian names. Not only have they been taken from their homes and the culture that they were used to, now they were given new names and told to eat things that were against what God wanted them to have. So, they purposed a plan to stay faithful to God and if you will check out verse 15 where it says; "And at the end of ten days their features appeared better and fatter in flesh than all the young men who ate the portion of the king's delicacies". We see that it worked out for them. And they served the king.

Later, the king builds an image of gold and told everybody in the nation that when they heard the sound of the horns, flute, harps and lyre in symphony, they were commanded to fall down and worship the golden image or be cast into the fiery furnace.

But these guys (most people know them by their Babylonian names as Shadrach, Meshach, and Abed-Nego) had been faithful to God and patient. They were not going to worship a golden image, because they knew the fifth commandment that God is a jealous God and didn't want them to bow down to a golden image.

We know that they refused the order of the king and would not bow to the golden image. The king gives them a chance and says, if you will just do as I say then you will be alright, but if you refuse, I will have to throw you into the furnace.

But they tell the king that they will stay faithful to God even if it costs them their lives. So, they throw them into the heat. The scripture says that the king got so upset that he even had them heat the furnace up so much that the guys that threw them into fire were burned up. But God shows up in the furnace.

Don't you love that about God, how He shows up when the heat is on? This king looks into the furnace and asks *"did we not* *cast three men bound into the midst of the fire?"* Then he says, *"look I see four men walking around loose in the furnace and the fourth is like the Son of God."* They were patient and waited and God delivered them from the fire.

And then awhile later in *Daniel 3:19-28,* we see Daniel, and a new king had taken over.

He liked Daniel, but he put out this decree that no man could petition any god for 30 days except for the king or be cast into the lion's den to be devoured. But Daniel like his three friends was not going to pray to, or worship, anyone or anything other than God. And although he had gained favor with this new king and the king tried not to follow the decree, he had to and cast Daniel into the lion's den.

I love the part when the king runs out to the lion's den the next morning and cries out to Daniel these beautiful words in *Daniel 6 "Daniel servant of the living God, has your God, whom you serve continually, been able to deliver you from the lions?"* And He had!

These four guys remained faithful to God and were patient and they were able to see His deliverance. And we can do the same thing today.

When the culture around us is telling us that we should do things that are against what God wants in our lives, we must remain faithful to Him and wait.

～

In 1994 my wife Sherri was having severe back pain. After many doctor visits we found out that she would need surgery to get relief, so she did. A few years later, she was in pain again, the fusion had broken lose and she again needed another surgery.

Unlike the first time, where she had a few years pain free, this time she didn't get relief. She struggled for three more years before having a third surgery at a different hospital, trying to get help. She had a couple years where she was better, but soon the pain came back. Now I don't want to tell you a lot of what we went through because the next book is going to be about that experience.

But I do want you to know that after 15 years of pain and trouble, God sent a doctor to us. After taking her all over the country to find help, He sent the doctor to our hometown. He fixed what was causing her pain and she is now better than she has been in years. But we had to trust that God was going to show up and **Wait For It**.

Chapter 4

Believe In Him

Believe In Him

Now I want us to look at a family that put themselves in **Position** to see Jesus work in their lives, but it wasn't easy for them. You see sometimes God allows things into our lives that aren't pleasant. Not only do we have to be in **position** to see Jesus, but we also must Believe in Him. Our story begins in; ***John 11:1-15*** Jesus knew that the cross was not too far away and that He would soon be facing death. He had moved to a safe place about a days walk from Bethany. Jesus got the word that His friend was sick and that they wanted Him to come to them. But by the time that word got to Jesus, His friend Lazarus was probably already dead. He waited two more days and then told the disciples *"Let's go to Judea".*

The disciples didn't want Jesus to go back there because of the anger the Jews there had toward Him.

They believed that this would be a suicide mission, and they had good reason to feel that way. Let's look at what had happened the last few days before this. In John chapter 8; in the story about the woman caught in adultery. Jesus tells them ***"I am the Light of the world".*** And in verse 25 of chapter 8 they ask, ***"who are you?".*** The last verse in that chapter it says, ***"they took up stones to throw at Him."*** And then in chapter 9 of the book of John, Jesus heals a man that was blind from birth on the Sabbath. The Pharisees got upset and threw the man out of the synagogue. Jesus found the man and ask him a very important question in verse 35 ***"Do you believe in the Son of God?".*** Chapter 10; Jesus says ***"I am the Good Shepherd"*** my sheep hear my voice and follow me.

Then the Jews confront Him at the temple and Jesus tells them that He is the Son of God. In verse 31 it says that ***"the Jews took up stones again to stone Him."***

In John chapter 11 verse 15 Jesus plainly tells the disciples the reason for the trip to Lazarus (So that they may Believe). Then in *John 11:16*, Thomas, one of His disciples, says something that I think is very interesting *"Let us also go, that we may die with Him."* Thomas and the other disciples knew that if they went back to Jerusalem with Jesus, they all might be killed, and they went anyway.

Are we willing to follow Jesus regardless of what may happen to us?

In *John 11:17-40,* we see that by the time they got to Bethany Lazarus had been dead 4 days.

The reason for the wait was that it was a custom in that time for people to go to the grave 3 days after burial and make sure the person was dead. So that had already happened. Lazarus was dead! I love the conversation that Jesus has with Martha.

She so much knew that Jesus could have saved Lazarus and she had some understanding of the resurrection. Jesus told her that He is the resurrection and life and ask her that very important question in verse 26 *"Do you believe?"* and her answer was a proclamation to the whole world. *"Yes, Lord, I believe that You are the Christ, the Son of God, who is to come into the world." John 11:27*

Do you believe in Jesus even when your world is turned upside down?

John 11:41-44, tells us that Jesus goes to the tomb and says roll the stone away, but they didn't want to because of the smell. And

Jesus asks Martha if she was in **position** to see Him move in her life? The 4-day wait is important to prove that this miracle could only be done by God Himself. This is the difference between this resurrection, and the others that Jesus had done.

It did three very important things.

1. It pointed to His deity.
2. It strengthened the faith of the disciples.
3. It led directly to the cross.

Do you want to see God at work in your life? Do you want to be in Position to witness His glory?

When our granddaughter was three years old, she got sick. She told my son that her stomach hurt and just laid around all weekend. They thought that she had a stomach virus of some kind and didn't take her to the doctor.

Early in the morning three days later, my son woke up in the middle of the night and just felt like he should check on her and when he did, he found her in really bad shape, so they rushed her to the hospital.

We found out that her appendix had ruptured and that she had infection all through her body, she was really in serious condition. They would have to do surgery soon or she would not make it. It was without a doubt one of the scariest times in our lives. The surgeon told us before the surgery that it didn't look good and that we needed to be prepared for the worst.

Sherri and I were devastated and cried out to God to help her because we felt like there was nothing else, we could do.

The Holy Spirit put in our hearts that we had to believe that God was going to take care of our beautiful granddaughter, regardless of how things turned out. And as hard as that was to do, we made a decision to trust Him, and we did.

After a month on a ventilator and four surgeries later, our sweet girl was released from the hospital and is doing great. We got to see God do a miracle in her life because we were in **Position** to **Believe in Him**.

Chapter 5

It Takes Faith

It Takes Faith

We are going to continue our look into, how to get ourselves into **position** to see God in our lives. We have already talked about how at times we need to just "Stand Back and Watch" like Jehoshaphat and the people of God did in *2 Chronicles*. And sometimes we need to "Put Some Effort Into It" like Zacchaeus did when he climbed that tree. At other times we should "Wait For It" like the four Hebrew boys in the book of Daniel. And in the last chapter we talked about how we must "Believe In Jesus" the way Martha did when Lazarus died.

Now we are going to see that "It Takes Faith". I would like to show you in scripture three things about a Roman Centurion that we can all learn from. In *Matthew 8:5-13* we see a man who is not a Jew.

He is a Roman Centurion, a captain of 100 men in the Roman army. The book of *Luke* tells us that *"he loved the nation of Israel and even built them a synagogue in Capernaum"*. This man knew about Jesus and had accepted Him as Lord. Therefore, when his servant got sick he came to Jesus. When he told Jesus about the servant Jesus offered to come to heal him, but the centurion humbled himself and told Him that he was unworthy for Jesus to be in his house. The first thing we should learn from this man is this.

1. He knew of his unworthiness.

Folks we all need to get to that point in our spiritual lives, to understand that we are unworthy to have Jesus. There is nothing we can do or have ever done that would make us worthy. Jesus comes into our lives because of His great love and compassion for us.

2. *He went himself.*

The second thing we can learn from him is he could have sent someone else to bring Jesus, but he didn't. Being a man of authority, he understood that Jesus also had authority and could command the healing of the servant whenever and however He wanted to. And when the centurion said these things to Jesus, the scriptures say that Jesus marveled at two things.

1. The great faith of this Gentile. V10
2. The unbelief of the Jews. V12

Does Jesus ever marvel at your Faith?
Or does He marvel at your unbelief?
This Roman soldier had the faith to know that Jesus could heal his friend without even being there.

The third thing we learn from him is that.

3. *He had great faith.*

The scripture says that the servant was healed that very hour. By coming to Jesus with faith and getting himself in **position**, this Roman soldier humbled himself and got to see God work a miracle in the life of his servant. Sometimes even when He does show up in our lives, we are so busy worrying about the problems that we have that we miss seeing Him. God is still the same now as he was then. He can still heal whenever He wants to. Will you have faith that Jesus will show up when you need Him?

~

A few years ago, Sherri and I started a small business. I had been driving a charter bus for a while to make some extra money and we decided to start our own bus tour business.

We were getting ready to go on a trip that required us to pay for everything a month before the trip date. We needed to have a certain number of people on the bus to make it profitable to go. Well, when the time came to pay we did not have enough people. We were seven people short, which meant that if I didn't pay, we could not go and the people we already had would be disappointed. If we did pay and didn't get the seven people we needed, then we would lose all the money we had paid.

So, we prayed about it and felt like we should go ahead and pay for everyone. We had to have faith that if God wanted us to do this business, then He would take care of it. That was a Wednesday morning and we had church that night. As I was teaching that night, my phone was vibrating in my pocket the whole time.

By the time we left the church I had forgotten how much it had happened until we were almost home.

I asked Sherri to look at my phone because someone had been trying to call me. When she did, we had messages from a couple of people and when we got home, I called them back and that night before we went to bed, we had exactly the number of people we needed to take the trip. We got to see God answer our prayer that same day. **Sometimes It Takes Faith**.

Chapter 6

Obedience is Required

Obedience Is Required

The Bible tells us that God can and will use some unlikely people to accomplish His will and we are going to learn about some of those people. I believe that there are some unlikely people in this world that God wants to use, even today, to lead people to Him. The first person we are going to learn about in the book of *Judges* is Gideon. But before we talk about him let me give you the context of what was going on with the children of Israel.

The children of Israel were doing evil in the sight of the Lord. Therefore, He had lifted His hand of protection from them, and they were being attacked by their enemies. The Midianites were desert bandits who came from the Arabian Desert to raid the farms of Israel.

They would attack the people of the valleys and steal the food and cattle, destroy the villages, and chase the Israelites into the hills. For seven years these bandits came back. Every time the Israelites were ready to reap the harvest, the Midianites came and stole the crops. The results were devastating. Again, this went on for seven years! Finally, the children of Israel were broken before God. They repented of their sin and cried out to God for deliverance.

Sometimes that same thing happens in our lives. We are His children, but we get ourselves out of **position** and do things that we know are against His will. And the next thing you know the enemy is attacking.

We first see Gideon in the book of *Judges 6:11-12.*

"Now the Angel of the LORD came and sat under the terebinth tree which *was* in Ophrah, which *belonged* to Joash the Abiezrite, while his son Gideon threshed wheat in the winepress, in order to hide *it* from the Midianites. [12] And the Angel of the LORD appeared to him, and said to him, "The LORD *is* with you, you mighty man of valor!"

God was planning on using the most unlikely person to be the hero of the nation. Gideon was down in a winepress trying to thresh wheat because he was afraid that if the <u>Midianites</u> saw him, they would come and steal his wheat. Usually a person would thresh his wheat out in the open on a threshing floor, but Gideon was trying to do it in a wine press.

I believe that fear is something that the enemy uses against Christians to keep them from doing what God wants them to do. Look at what Gideon says in verse 13 *"If the Lord is with us, why then has all this happened to us? Where are all His miracles that we heard about?"*

Gideon had given up on God. But doesn't this sound a lot like us sometimes? We're going through a trial of some kind, and we ask that same question; "Why is this happening to me?"

You see Gideon's real enemy was not just the Midianites; it was Fear, Insecurity, Doubt, and Unbelief. Brothers and sisters these are the same enemies that each and every one of us faces today. Look at what it says in *Judges 6:14-15*

When the angel of the Lord spoke to Gideon, he (Gideon) started coming up with as many excuses he could come up with to talk his way out of doing what God wanted him to do. *"My family is the weakest in the group, and I'm the least in my father's house."* Basically, he is saying "God I'm not your man for this job. Get somebody else to do it," But God has a way of choosing the most unlikely candidates to do His work. But the answer that God had for him is.

"Surely I will be with you."

Folks we can rest in this truth in our lives today. When we fight against the enemies of Fear, Insecurity, Doubt and Unbelief we can know that with God we can be triumphant.

The Bible tells us in **Romans 8:31** that *"if God is for us, who can be against us?"*

The next verses talk about how Gideon asks God for a sign to show that it really was Him asking him to do this thing. And the angel of the Lord did what he asks Him to do and gave him the sign. Then God told him to tear down the alter of Baal and build an alter to God in its place and sacrifice on it. And Gideon is obedient and does as the Lord ask of him, but it says in verse 27 that he was also afraid of *"the men of the city."*

Gideon was still fighting that enemy called Fear. As soon as Gideon took a stand for what was right, people lined up to follow him. God took the most unlikely person imaginable, touched his life, and empowered him to be all God wanted him to be. When we are **obedient** to God and **position** ourselves to be used by Him, then He will touch our lives and use us to bring glory to Him.

People came from all the surrounding towns and all the northern tribes saying, **"We're here to follow you!"** Then fear took over his life again and he ask for another sign from God.

When all was said and done Gideon had an army of 32,000 men. The problem was there were 130,000 Midianites and Amalekites down in the valley. Gideon must have thought to himself, *we're outnumbered! We don't stand a chance! We're doomed! What am I going to do?* God then spoke to Gideon and said, "We've got a problem." *"You've got too many men."*

God told Gideon he had too many men and started thinning

out the crowd. First, he took out the ones who were afraid. That left 10,000. It is said that in any army there are three kinds of people in a battle. First, they say is anybody with any sense was afraid, and that covered most people.

That's why two-thirds of Gideon's army left. Second, there was a bunch of guys who just wanted to fight. They didn't care if they got killed. They would stay and fight. Most of the other third of Gideon's army was probably like them. Then there was a third category of men in battle. They were too afraid to admit that they were afraid. These guys were so afraid that when Gideon said, *"raise your hand, if you are afraid."* They couldn't even raise their hands. They were too afraid to admit that they were afraid.

Now we have the ones I like to call the Lappers, the **300** men who were Gideon's army. In *Judges 7:5-7* it says;

"So he brought the people down to the water. And the LORD said to Gideon, "Everyone who laps from the water with his tongue, as a dog laps, you shall set apart by himself; likewise everyone who gets down on his knees to drink."

[6] And the number of those who lapped, *putting* their hand to their mouth, was three hundred men; but all the rest of the people got down on their knees to drink water. [7] Then the LORD said to Gideon, "By the three hundred men who lapped I will save you, and deliver the Midianites into your hand. Let all the *other* people go, every man to his place."

We can see that God tested the remaining people to see who would fight. Those who got down and drank from the water with his tongue were the guys I said were not afraid to die. They didn't look around while they were drinking. They were not worried about the enemy coming after them.

The ones who swooped the water up into their hands and

lapped it while at the same time keeping watch were afraid. They were the ones too afraid to even admit that they were. These are the unlikely people that God is going to use to deliver the children of Israel from the Midianites.

The Lord gave Gideon an incredible battle plan. He told him to take the three hundred men and divide them into three groups. He gave instructions to Gideon to give a pitcher with a torch inside it to every man and a trumpet for them to carry. Then He told him to put a hundred men on each side of the valley and a hundred in the middle. Gideon was to give the signal and the men would break the pitchers, wave the torches, and blow on the trumpets.

Then they were to shout, *"The sword of the Lord and Gideon!"* In the middle of the night Gideon's enemies heard the smashing of the pottery pitchers. It simulated the clash of arms and echoed down the valley below.

The noise terrified the Midianites and Amalekites. They looked up and saw the torches and heard the trumpets surrounding their camp. They assumed there were thousands of soldiers. They panicked, thinking that the Israelites had hired allies to come against them.

In the confusion of the noise and darkness the two groups of people slaughtered each other without even realizing it. Before the night was over, 120,000 Midianites and Amalekites were dead. All Gideon and his 300 men had to do was be **obedient** and make some noise for God!

So how about you? Will you get out and make some noise for God? Will you let your light shine so bright in this dark world that the enemy would turn and run, in fear?

Or are you going to continue to let the enemy stop you? I'm ready to make some noise! How about you?

~

The first church that I was called to Pastor was a small one. The first Sunday we went there, we had nine people show up.

And it seemed like things just went downhill from there. After a while they decided to have a meeting about closing the church and giving up.

Sherri and I both felt like this is where God wanted us to be, and we were trying our best to be obedient to Him. So, during the meeting I expressed this to the people that were there. I told them I knew that God would open another door for us if they decided to close the church.

At the meeting was my only deacon and his wife, and she stood up and told all of us very plainly that she believed God wanted the church to remain open and that she was against the thought of closing.

Well, when she said that, I could feel the Holy Spirit telling me to join with her and I did. We kept the church open and all of us got to see God move in miraculous ways.

People started showing up, the deacons wife's cousin the first week and her daughter the next. And over and over again, every week someone new came. We were baptizing people and others would come. People were giving to the church. We had money in the bank and people in the pews. It was one of the most amazing things to watch as God grew **His** church. We all learned that if we want to see God at work, **Obedience Is Required.**

Chapter 7

Even When Trials Come

Even When Trials Come

Trials come on all of us. Sometimes it could be physical, financial, relational, emotional or spiritual. Things happen in life that are sometimes hard. But when this happens, we still want to keep ourselves in a **position** to where we can see God move. The older I get the more I realize that the people I come into contact with everyday have trials in their lives, they may not show it on the outside, but on the inside they are hurting. In this chapter, we are going to look at some people in scripture that are going through a trial, yet they **positioned** themselves where they could see God.

In the book of Acts we can read about the Apostle Paul and his many missionary journeys; he went from town to town starting churches and preaching about Jesus.

Along the way he teamed up with a fellow called Silas, and they were led by the Holy Spirit to go to Macedonia. To a city called Philippi. In *Acts 16:16-24* Paul and Silas were going to a prayer service and they were followed by a girl who was possessed by an evil spirit. This girl would tell people's fortunes and that made her owners a lot of money in the process. I want us to see three things about this girl whom Paul and Silas met.
1st- She was a slave.

She belonged to people who were making money from her ability to contact demons that supposedly helped her predict the future.

2nd- She was possessed by an evil spirit.

With a spirit of divination. She was a medium, someone who was supposed to be able to tell the future, a fortune teller.

3rd- She had knowledge of the truth.

The things that she cried out to everyone for many days was the truth. These men were servants of the Most High God, and they did proclaim the way of salvation.

She was probably saying it in a mocking or sarcastic way. Whatever was the reason Paul got tired of hearing her and demanded the evil spirit to come out of her. And it did, setting her free. The people who owned her realized that they had lost their way of using her and got upset. They grabbed Paul and Silas and had them beat with a stick and put them in jail with their feet in stocks. But look at what Paul and Silas did in Acts 16:25

"But at midnight Paul and Silas were praying and singing hymns to God, and the prisoners were listening to them."

Instead of feeling sorry for themselves or having a pity party, they give God praise.

Paul and Silas, even through a difficult trial remained faithful to God and sang praises and lifted prayers to Him in the jail and God showed up.

A great earthquake happened, and I love how it says all the doors were opened and everyone's chains were loosed. Folks, when we keep ourselves in **position** to see God at work, those around us will benefit from it.

Everyone was set free, yet none escaped. The jailer, thinking that everyone had escaped was getting ready to kill himself instead of facing the consequences of all his prisoners escaping. Then Paul called out to him *"we are all here"*. Seeing what God had done for Paul and Silas, this man asked the question that many people need to ask today *"what must I do to be saved"*.

And Paul gave him the same answer that we should give people today *"believe on the Lord Jesus Christ"*. Our scriptures say that he and his household were baptized, and he rejoiced.

Do you see what happens when we stay in the **position** to see God at work even when going through a hard time?

These guys could have gotten upset, they could have blamed God. After all they were just trying to spread the Good News, yet they were beaten and thrown in jail. They could have had a pity party and gripped and complained, but they didn't. They praised God even in the hard times and He delivered them from the trial. This is just one story of many where Paul had to trust God and stay faithful in a hard time.

Look at what he writes to his friend Timothy in

2 Timothy 4:7

"I have fought the good fight, I have finished the race, I have kept the faith."

Paul put himself in **position** to finish the race, he kept the faith. How about you? Do you have yourself in **position** to finish the race?

As I finish this race called writing a book and I think about this last chapter about trials. It dawned on me just how many I have faced in my life. So many that I couldn't even think about which one I wanted to write about. Would it be, when we were going through Sherri's back trouble. Maybe when our granddaughter was going through her illness.

Or when God had to carry us through a financial issue (which has happened too many times to remember)? Life is just hard sometimes. We just need to remember that God **will** show up and we will be able to see Him do miraculous things **Even When Trials Come**.

The End

About the Author

Johnny and Sherri live in a small town in Central Kentucky. Where he is the Pastor of Pleasant Hill Baptist Church. They have been married for over 40 years. They have two grown sons and three grandchildren. Although he has journaled for many years, this is his first book.

Printed in the United States
by Baker & Taylor Publisher Services